SPY, SPY AGAIN

True Tales of Failed Espionage

SPY, SPY AGAIN

True Tales of Failed Espionage

WRITTEN AND ILLUSTRATED BY TINA HOLDCROFT

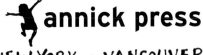

annick press

TORONTO • NEW YORK • VANCOUVER

THIS BOOK IS BRILLIANTLY BUNCHED INTO **5** BUNGLING
CHAPTERS.

INTRODUCTION

WARNING!

This is a nasty little book. It's all about real life flubs, fumbles, and bungles in the murky old world of espionage. Yes, it's a book about SPY FAILURE. Mwahaahaaa …

No one ever said that spying was easy. Folks have been botching plots for well over 3,000 years. Historians figure that spies have been slipping up much longer than that but, darn it, those ancient cave dwellers and dead old cultures never kept records, so we don't have a sneaky spy clue about them. But once the ancients started to write about themselves, watch out! Bring on the blunders.

Funny thing is, from ancient times to now, folks have hired spies for the same old reason: to get a head — I mean … get ahead. Military leaders have always depended on spies to see what's up with their enemy (new weapons, troop positions, and whatnot). Government leaders have regularly used espionage to keep an eye on any threats to their power or their people. And big businesses have snooped to get the inside poop about their competitors. Then everyone has used their spies' information to make informed and (they hope) winning decisions.

But, uh-ohh, spy schemes don't always go to plan. There are so many ways to mess up. And the consequences of failed espionage plots can be nasty, nasty, nasty — for the both the spies and their bosses. But do worries of failure stop folks from snooping? No! They just make new plans and spy, spy again.

What follows? This book, of course. Presenting 20 botched and bungled spy jobs from around the globe. Enjoy.

CHAPTER 1
OOPS!

You have to be such a fusspot, a nitpicker ... a perfectionist to plan a successful spy mission. After all, your enemies aren't stupid — they're on the lookout for your secret agents.

WE'VE SPENT MONTHS PREPARING FOR THIS MISSION. NOTHING CAN GO WRONG.

So with meticulous planning, you carefully select the perfect spies for the job, give them specific training if necessary — and provide the spies with props and specialized equipment too. Oh — I almost forgot — you will also come up with a stunningly cunning plan to get your agents close to the enemy target without arousing suspicions. Organizing this lot takes a great deal of time, hard work, and resources. Phew!

Ready now? Every last detail sorted? Good. But I should warn you, there's one little thing that your perfect plan will never be prepared for. It's called BAD LUCK.

Oops!

ANTS ENCOUNTER

AN ANTSY END IN ANCIENT INDIA

SPY-SCHOOL DROPOUTS

WWII SPY STUDENTS MISS THE MARK.

PARABLOOPERS

THE DOWNFALL OF A WWII SPY MISSION

SUNKEN SUNKEN SOVIET SUB

A COLOSSAL COLD WAR SLIPUP

ANTS ENCOUNTER

Ants give ancient Indian spies crummy luck.

OK. Forget about ants for a second. Here's the big picture. Things were hopping in the sub continent of India over 2,300 years ago. Before 323 BCE, the place was a mix of kingdoms and tribal territories with the top northwest corner lorded over by pesky foreigners — the ancient Greeks. But all that changed when a young man called Chandragupta Maurya jumped into the jumble.

Around 323 BCE, Chandragupta Maurya not only kicked a king off the throne of India's biggest kingdom but he also had a friendly chat with the foreigners in the northwest. They moved out and Chandragupta moved in.

Emperor Chandragupta then went on to unify a huge chunk of the subcontinent, creating the mighty MAURYA EMPIRE.

But what about those ants? And spies? Well, one of the ancient Indian and Greek documents that focussed on these historical figures and their times is an Indian drama called the *Mudrarakshasa,* which historians love to study. Much of ancient history comes to us from these types of sources, which show us the ideas and culture of the day, though without necessarily depicting historic events.

And, yes, the *Mudrarakshasa* tells of an antique espionage antic, involving . . . ants.

8

Is there a great spy lesson to be learned here? Not really. Other than don't be a messy eater— you really can't anticipate crummy luck.

Chandragupta survived the spy attacks. The Maurya Empire grew even wealthier and more powerful under the leadership of his son and his super-famous grandson, Ashoka. A golden age in Indian art, religion, the sciences, and philosophy all blossomed during the Mauryan era, which ended in 185 BCE.

Chanakya went on to write two really famous books: the *Arthashastra* (mostly about how to run an empire) and the *Neetishastra* (advice on how to live an ideal and moral life).

SPY-SCHOOL DROPOUTS

Shhhh . . . A World War II spy school has an inconvenient problem.

You know all about World War II, right? When, back in the last century, most of the world took sides in the biggest, bloodiest war in human history? From 1939 to 1945 experts estimate that over 50 million people perished.

In 1940, when France fell to the enemy (the Germans), the United Kingdom (France's ally) quickly created a new volunteer fighting force called the Special Operations Executive (SOE). Specially trained SOE agents were asked to tiptoe into enemy occupied territories such as poor old France and commit artful acts like sabotage (blowing up bridges, trains, and factories, etc.) and subversion (assisting folks to resist, revolt, and cause major mayhem for their enemy landlords). Dangerous work.

The SOE carefully chose the men and women for these highly specialized missions and sent them off to spy schools for intensive training. But not everyone got a passing grade, which was darned . . . inconvenient.

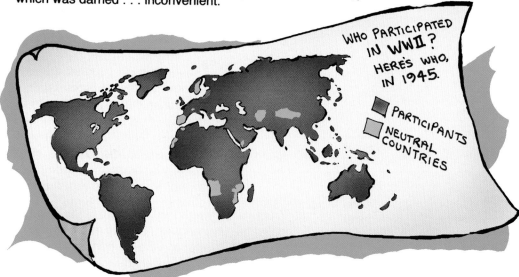

THE SOE EXPECTED THEIR SPIES TO DO A NASTY JOB.

TAKE EDDIE CHAPMAN (AGENT ZIGZAG), FOR EXAMPLE — ONE OF BRITAIN'S MOST IMPORTANT DOUBLE AGENTS OF WWII.

I CONVINCED THE GERMANS THAT I WOULD SPY FOR THEM BUT I DOUBLE CROSSED THEM AND GAVE FALSE INFORMATION.

EDDIE CHAPMAN'S CRIMINAL RECORD · · · · · · · ·
○ BLACKMAILER
○ SAFECRACKER
○ THIEF
— WAS SERVING A 15-YEAR PRISON SENTENCE IN BRITAIN'S CHANNEL ISLANDS WHEN THE GERMANS TOOK OVER.

THE SOE MADE THEIR CHOICE.

ZIGZAG WORKED UNDER BRITAIN'S MAIN INTELLIGENCE AGENCY — THE MI5.

THE SOE SENT THE WANNA-BE SPIES TO A 4-DAY WORKSHOP TO SEE IF THE VOLUNTEERS WERE MENTALLY AND PHYSICALLY UP FOR THE JOB. (BEFORE JUNE 1948 THIS WAS DONE AT THE PRELIMINARY SCHOOL.)

GASP!

THE CHOSEN ONES ENTERED A 4-STAGE TRAINING PROGRAM.

YEP, IT'S SCHOOL TIME!

1 PRELIMINARY SCHOOL
WHERE STUDENTS LEARNED THE BASICS
● WEAPONS HANDLING
● DEMOLITION 101
● FIELD CRAFT
● PHYSICAL TRAINING
● UNARMED COMBAT
● MAP READING
● BASIC SIGNALS

WHEEZE.

ERRP.

PUFF, PANT.

RUN!

UG

WELCOME TO SPY SCHOOL. MAKE YOURSELVES COMFORTABLE.

THE SOE USED LUXURY MANOR HOUSES, SHOOTING LODGES, COUNTRY ESTATES, AND EVEN A CASTLE FOR THE TRAINING SCHOOLS. STUDENTS JOKED THAT SOE MEANT STATELY 'OMES OF ENGLAND.

WAIT THERE'S MORE

THE PRELIMINARY SCHOOL GRADUATES MOVED ONTO THE NEXT TRAINING STAGE.

2 PARAMILITARY SCHOOL
...WHERE STUDENTS JUMPED INTO THE NASTY STUFF

- HOW TO BLOW UP SHIPS
- PARACHUTE TRAINING
- FITNESS TRAINING
- SILENT KILLING
- RAID TACTICS
- AND MORE

ARGHH!

...SEE? NOT A SOUND. WHO'S NEXT?

3 FINISHING SCHOOL
HERE, THE SOE FINALLY TOLD THE STUDENTS THAT THEY WERE TRAINING TO BE SPIES. (MOST HAD GUESSED BY NOW ANYWAY.)

HOW TO:
- STEAL
- MAINTAIN YOUR SPY COVER
- PICK LOCKS AND HANDCUFFS
- USE CODES, CIPHERS, AND SECRET INKS

HOW TO ACT IF:
- YOU'RE BEING WATCHED BY THE POLICE
- YOU'RE ARRESTED AND BEING INTERROGATED

GASP!

...SO, IF THEY TORTURE YOU...

TRY NOT TO BLAB.

4 SPECIALIST SCHOOL
SOME MISSIONS NEEDED SPECIAL TRAINING.

- ADVANCED MICRO PHOTOGRAPHY
- HOW TO USE ENEMY WEAPONS
- MAKING EXPLOSIVE DEVICES

HOW TO ATTACK:
- RAILWAY LINES AND TRAINS
- BERTHED SUBMARINES
- GROUNDED AIRCRAFT
- FACTORY MACHINERY
- NON-MILITARY SHIPS AND DOCKS

IN BRITAIN, THE SOE PROVIDED SOME 13,500 COURSES TO TEACH 6,800 STUDENTS.

GASP! SO MUCH TO REMEMBER.

SHHH... JUST SO YOU KNOW... NOT ALL SPY SCHOOLS WERE IN BRITAIN. CANADA'S **CAMP X** WAS NORTH AMERICA'S FIRST WWII SPY SCHOOL.

ALL 4 STAGES OF TRAINING DONE HERE

CAMP X TRAINED
- FRENCH CANADIANS
- ENGLISH CANADIANS
- LOADS OF AMERICANS AND REFUGEES

BUILT ON ONTARIO FARMLAND

BOOM!
BANG!

PHEW!
HARD WORK.

BUT THOUGH THE SPY STUDENTS WERE CAREFULLY CHOSEN

SOME STUDENTS GOT A FAILING GRADE.

WHIMPER.

HAD A RE-THINK

UNABLE TO KILL

GRUMBLE.

ROTTEN ATTITUDE

AND SOMETIMES FOR THE STRANGEST REASONS.

TOO UGLY

OOPS.

HE PASSED ALL HIS COURSES — HE'S A GOOD MAN

YES, BUT LOOK AT THOSE TEETH.

HE'LL ATTRACT TOO MUCH ATTENTION WHEREVER HE GOES.

THESE FAILED SPY STUDENTS GAVE THE SOE MAJOR HEADACHES.

BLAST! HE KNOWS TOO MUCH ABOUT OUR TOP-SECRET PLANS NOW.

HE COULD JEOPARDIZE THE WHOLE MISSION IF HE TALKED.

OOPS! A SECURITY RISK!

SO...

HOW DID THE SOE SHUSH THOSE SPY-SCHOOL DROPOUTS WHO KNEW TOO MUCH?

NO, NOT KILL THEM, YOU EVIL-MINDED READERS! IT'S NOT NICE TO NIX VOLUNTEERS.

INVERLAIR LUXURY LODGE

WELCOME TO YOUR NEW "HOME" LADDIE

BAAA.

Yes, just like the sign says, the failed spies who knew too much were taken to Inverlair Lodge in the wilds of Scotland, where they wiled away their days in the lap of luxury on this huge estate. Though they were allowed to visit a nearby village, this secret fancy detention camp prevented the spy-school dropouts from coming into contact with the wider world and possibly spilling any SOE secrets. Successful spies who were a security risk to the Allies were also "invited" to stay there too. Tea and crumpets, anyone?

This luxurious wartime prison was the inspiration for a 1967 – 68 television series and a 2009 movie, both called *The Prisoner*.

PARABLOOPERS

**Sending spies into Germany…
What could possibly go wrong?**

We're still in World War II here, but it's getting close to the end. By September 1944, it looked like the Allies were winning the war in Europe. The German military had been pushed out of many lands that they had previously occupied in a series of bloody battles. Everyone hoped that the war would be over by Christmas. But the Germans wouldn't give up. They stiffened their defenses and carried on fighting. Britain's prime minister finally said, "The truth is no one knows when the Germans will be finished."

America's intelligence agency, the Office of Strategic Services (OSS), decided to send spies inside Germany to see how strong or weak the German military and defenses really were. Not an easy task as the Gestapo (Nazi Germany's secret police) had done a thorough job of wiping out any pockets of resistance inside Germany. This meant that no one could meet the spies and hide them when they arrived.

Careful planning and preparations for these difficult missions was dead important. But so many things could go wrong …

OOOPS!

UG.

WHAT'S HAPPENING INSIDE GERMANY?

NO IDEA.

SEND IN THE SPIES.

EUROPE

GERMANY ?

GERMAN-CONTROLLED LAND THAT THE ALLIES FREED IN 1944

JUNE–JULY

JULY–SEPTEMBER

SEPTEMBER–DECEMBER

BUT OHH...THE TRANSPORTATION PROBLEMS.

LOW, SLOW BOMBERS FLEW THE AGENTS INTO GERMANY.

WE'RE 32 KILOMETERS (20 MILES) OFF OUR TARGET.

START WALKING.

THOUGH THE DROP SPOTS WERE CAREFULLY CONSIDERED...

THE SPIES DIDN'T ALWAYS DROP ON THE SPOT.

BAM!

SOME FLIGHT CREWS WERE MORE EXPERIENCED AND MORE ACCURATE THAN OTHERS.

ARGH!

SOMETIMES STRONG WINDS BLEW THE PARACHUTES OFF COURSE.

BOOF!

LANDING WITHIN HALF A MILE (800 METERS) WAS A GOOD DROP.

POW!

LOCATING THE DROP-OFF SPOT IN THE DARK WAS TRICKY.

BOOM!

LOW CLOUDS OR FOG MADE THE JOB EVEN HARDER.

BANG!

FLAK (EXPLOSIVES FROM ANTI-AIRCRAFT GUNS) WAS NO PICNIC EITHER.

YOU WILL PARACHUTE HERE TONIGHT.

THAT LOOKS LOVELY.

AND NOW... **THE BIG OOPS**

Mission Code Name: Pitt
Date: January 2, 1945
Objective: To spy on the German army division posted in the Black Forest

GERMAN TROOPS

BLACK FOREST

KARLSRUHE

PLASTER MODEL OF THE AREA

19

So what happened next? Usually spies caught red-handed like these two would be executed pretty darned quickly, but, luckily, the spies had a radio.

The Germans "requested" that they transmit false information to the OSS. The radioman agreed but sent a warning signal to the OSS by spelling his name Karl instead of the Americanized Carl.

The OSS sent back a steady stream of true but useless intelligence called "chicken feed," which kept the spies alive until the Allied troops overtook that part of Germany later in the year.

SUNKEN SOVIET SUB

**The plan is bold, the payoff big.
But can the plot get botched?**

Diving right into this next story, in March 1968, a submarine from the Soviet Union sank to the seafloor some 5 kilometers (3 miles) below the surface, taking all its sailors down with it.

You'd think that a sunken submarine would be the end of the story, but it was just the beginning. For though it was peacetime when the sub sank, it had been armed with three ballistic missiles with nuclear warheads, which were ready to be launched at the United States of America should war break out. Chilling stuff. What was going on?

Here's what. After the heated battles of World War II, which ended in 1945, global politics sunk into an icy era. That's when the USA and the Soviet Union started behaving mistrustfully, competitively, and downright frostily toward each other. Did I mention sneakily too?

These two enemy superpowers developed and built nuclear weapons of mass destruction at an alarming rate, making the world a darned jittery place to live in. Diplomats worked overtime to stop the threats from heating up, calling this whole chilling era, (which finally defrosted in 1991) the Cold War.

So what's the low down on this Cold War sunken submarine? The USA was so curious to see what lay inside the sub that they plunged into a deeply sneaky and plucky plot.

THE BEGINNING...

MARCH 1968

...AFTER A SOVIET SUBMARINE TOOK ITS FINAL DIP

...AND THE SOVIET NAVY GAVE UP SEARCHING THE SEAFLOOR WITH SONAR

WE HAVE NO IDEA WHERE TO LOOK.

PING PING PING

AND AFTER THE US NAVY FOUND THE SUNKEN SUB WITH SOSUS

WE'RE PICKING UP LOTS OF NOISE. IT SOUNDS LIKE THE SOVIETS HAVE LOST A SUBMARINE.

SEARCH THE RECORDS AND FIND THAT SUB.

SOSUS — THE USA'S SOUND SURVEILLANCE SYSTEM

A CHAIN OF UNDERWATER LISTENING POSTS IN THE PACIFIC AND ATLANTIC OCEANS THAT TRACKED SOVIET SUBMARINES.

SOME FOLKS IN THE USA GOT DEEPLY EXCITED...

...AND FORMED A DARINGLY BOLD SPY MISSION.

WHAT A SUPER OPPORTUNITY TO CHECK OUT THE SOVIETS' SECRET STUFF!

DEPARTMENT OF DEFENSE

AMERICA'S SPY GUYS —THE CIA (CENTRAL INTELLIGENCE AGENCY)

OOO-OOO WHY DON'T WE RAISE THE SUB!

CHECK OUT THE SOVIETS' TECHNOLOGY,

NUCLEAR MISSILE CAPABILITIES

CODE BOOKS...

STRATEGIES

MANUALS

TRANSMITTERS

TOP SECRET

July 1, 1969

CIA PROJECT AZORIAN

THE OBJECTIVE: TO SOMEHOW RECOVER THE SUBMARINE ...SOMEHOW

...IN COMPLETE AND UTTER SECRECY

!

THEY'RE GOING TO PICK UP A 1,750-TON SUBMARINE THAT'S LYING 5 KILOMETERS (3 MILES) DOWN ON THE SEAFLOOR?

THIS CALLS FOR THE MOST AMBITIOUS OCEAN-ENGINEERING VENTURE EVER ATTEMPTED BY MAN. IN TERMS OF TECHNOLOGICAL ACHIEVEMENT, THIS MUST BE COMPARED TO THE FIRST MOON LANDING (1969).

23

24

MEANWHILE THE *GLOMAR EXPLORER* LOWERED CLEMENTINE FROM THE "MOON POOL" COMPARTMENT INSIDE THE SHIP...

BOLTING LENGTH AFTER LENGTH OF PIPE STRINGS TOGETHER TO DROP THE VEHICLE DOWN TO THE WRECK SITE.

MOON POOL

CLEMENTINE

GOT IT!

CLEMENTINE'S CLAWS CAREFULLY GRABBED THE SUNKEN SUB.

ON AUGUST 1, THE *GLOMAR EXPLORER'S* GIANT WINCHES BEGAN PULLING UP THE SUB.

OF COURSE, THE SOVIET TUG BOAT COULDN'T SEE A THING.

AUGUST 6, 1974 THE SOVIETS SAILED AWAY.

BYE-BYE

PHEW! GOODBYE TO 13 DAYS AND 16 HOURS OF SURVEILLANCE.

...3 DAYS LATER AUGUST 9, 1974 THE SOVIET SUB WAS PULLED INSIDE THE *GLOMAR EXPLORER'S* MOON POOL ... THEN SUDDENLY

OH Nooooo.

OOPS!

BAD LUCK!

GROAN

EQUIPMENT FAILURE

RRRIP

BOTCHED

K129

MOST OF THE SUB TORE AWAY FROM CLEMENTINE'S CLAWS AND PLUMMETED DOWN TO THE SEAFLOOR.

WHAT WAS RECOVERED IN THE SURVIVING SECTION OF THE SUB? THE BODIES OF 6 SOVIET SAILORS. IS THAT ALL?

The CIA is staying silent about the rest, but informed accounts say that the sub's nuclear torpedoes survived in the remaining portion of the submarine but NOT the nuclear missiles, NOT the code books, NOT the manuals and NOT the transmitters. In fact, everything that the CIA really wanted to see had just disintegrated into little pieces on the sea floor. The CIA did NOT go back down to pick them up. What was the cost of this big, bold, and botched spy mission? $500 million (in 1974 dollars).

CHAPTER 2
SAY WHAT?

Yes ... we all know that communicating means sharing information, but, listen, in the slippery, sly world of espionage, you can't always count on your spy's communications and that's the truth.

But your war, your business, or your security can easily fizzle with incorrect information. So do your darndest to dodge these no-nos.

DISINFORMATION: Lies all lies! It's deliberately incorrect information. Someone is trying to mislead you.
MISINFORMATION: Incorrect information again, but it's accidental. Your spy made a mistake.
MISCOMMUNICATION: Once again, incorrecto. The information was either lost or misunderstood because you or your spy were unclear.

Got that? Course you did. You and I communicate just fine. Say what?

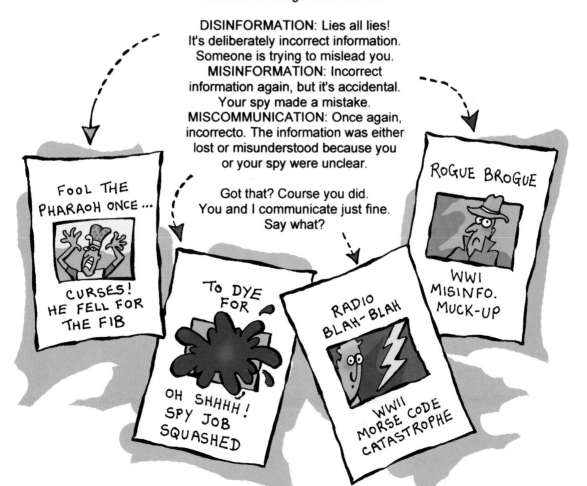

FOOL THE PHARAOH ONCE ...
CURSES! HE FELL FOR THE FIB

TO DYE FOR
OH SHHHH! SPY JOB SQUASHED

RADIO BLAH-BLAH
WWII MORSE CODE CATASTROPHE

ROGUE BROGUE
WWI MISINFO. MUCK-UP

FOOL THE PHARAOH ONCE...

Lying spies almost make a mummy out of the pharaoh.

What's the pharaoh saying here? Relax, all you grown-ups, he's muttering "blast," though he probably turned the sand blue with curses when he realized that history's biggest chariot battle ever recorded was about to be mucked up by a cunningly clever lie (disinformation) and some sneaky old spies.

Way back in the year 1274 BCE, two empires clashed over a chunk of land in ancient Syria. This land used to belong to the Egyptian empire, but the Hittite empire (originating from ancient Turkey) had nibbled away at Egypt's borderlands and had taken over the huge city-state of Kadesh.

Egypt's ambitious young pharaoh, Ramses II (third ruler of Egypt's 19th dynasty of the prosperous New Kingdom), had been sitting on the throne for 5 years, when he finally decided that enough was enough! Darn it, he was going to get rid of those annoying land-stealing Hittites once and for all and reclaim Egypt's land.

But the Hittites' King Muwatalli was no pushover. . .

IN THE SPRING OF **1274 BCE,** **RAMSES** AND HIS ARMY MARCHED NORTH TO SYRIA. THE OBJECTIVE: TO KICK THOSE LAND-GRABBING HITTITES OFF EGYPTIAN TERRITORIES.

OUR ARMY IS HUGE! WE CAN'T LOSE.

20,000 FOOT SOLDIERS. 2,000 NEW ULTRA-LIGHT AND SPEEDY CHARIOTS. PLUS 5,000 ELITE SOLDIERS FROM VASSAL LANDS.

RAMSES LED THE WAY WITH HIS AMUN BATTALION.

THE ARMY WAS DIVIDED INTO 4 BATTALIONS NAMED AFTER EGYPTIAN GODS: AMUN, RE, SETH, AND PTAH.

BUT... **MUWATALLI** KING OF THE **HITTITES** WAS MORE THAN READY FOR RAMSES.

KING MUWATALLI MUSTERED AN EVEN BIGGER ARMY WITH TROOPS FROM 19 ALLIED LANDS.

37,000 FOOT SOLDIERS. 2,500 TO 3,500 HEAVY CHARIOTS.

WHILE THE EGYPTIANS MARCHED CLOSER TO THE HITTITE-HELD CITY OF **KADESH,** MUWATALLI CUNNINGLY PLOTTED WAYS TO IMPROVE HIS ODDS OF WINNING.

BOTH SIDES KNOW WE WILL BE FIGHTING HERE AT KADESH, BUT I WANT OUR ATTACK TO BE A COMPLETE SURPRISE.

YOU TWO—GO AND SPY ON THE EGYPTIANS' TROOP MOVEMENTS.

AND I NEED YOU TWO TO SPREAD A LITTLE DISINFORMATION.

Who won history's first fully documented war and likely the biggest chariot battle of ancient times? After much blood, guts, and gore, the two armies declared a truce. Ramses' Egyptian army left with Muwatalli's Hittite army still in control of Kadesh.

But according to ancient Egyptian hieroglyphs about the Battle of Kadesh, you'd think that the Egyptians won outright. A surviving Hittite account says otherwise. Historians call it a draw.

Just as in military campaigns today, both sides used strategy, scouts, spies, and lies to give themselves the edge. Who knows what would have happened if those captured Hittites hadn't tattled. But we do know that disinformation gave the Hittites the first advantage and almost made a mummy out of Ramses before his time.

Ramses II lived to a ripe old age and reigned for another 66 years. He is considered to be one of the greatest pharaohs of all.

To DYE FOR

The quirky quest for Spain's secret red

See those splotches? They're color samples for textile dyes and that bottom splat was once such a huge moneymaker that it sparked over 200 years of industrial espionage (spying for economic reasons). It even sent one spy into a red rage after a miscommunication disaster. What a washout! But why all the fuss over a color? At one time, red dyes were so darned expensive and difficult to make that only the rich folk of Europe could ever afford to wear clothes made with them.

So imagine the surprise when those Spanish conquistadors strolled through the marketplaces of the Americas (the New World) not long after Europe's Christopher Columbus first set foot on the continent in 1492 and saw red. Hard not to miss. The market-places sold piles of fabrics and feathers, dyed with a brilliant red, so rarely seen in Europe, plus heaps of red dye that the locals called cochineal.

In the early 1500s, after the Spanish conquered ancient Mexico, sacks of the dyestuff were shipped back home to Spain. And as you can guess, Europe went wild over the new red. Textile dyers scooped the stuff up and the Spanish made a killing.

But what exactly was this cochineal dye? Merchants were dead curious and green with envy. They wanted to get rich too! But of course, Spain closely guarded this super money-making secret. If you're dyeing … I mean dying to know more, read on.

RED MADDER MADE FROM PLANT ROOTS

DYE MADE FROM BRAZIL WOOD BUT IT FADES FAST

ONLY 3 KNOWN RED DYES WERE MADE FROM INSECTS, BUT THEY WERE HARD AND EXPENSIVE TO MAKE.

COCHINEAL RED THE STRONGEST AND BRIGHTEST DYE THAT THE OLD WORLD HAD EVER SEEN

THEY'RE DYING TO KNOW OUR SECRET.

SPAIN

OLD WORLD

NEW WORLD

MEXICO

■ SPANISH EMPIRE (1770)

THIS STORY STARTED IN **MEXICO**.

FEMALE COCHINEAL

ACTUAL SIZE

NEEDS NOPAL CACTUS (PRICKLY PEAR) TO SURVIVE

LIVES UNDER FUZZY WHITE SCALE

THE COCHINEAL CAME FROM HERE

MEXICO

WE SELL OUR DYESTUFF TO THE SPANISH.

LONG AGO... INSTEAD OF GATHERING COCHINEAL IN THE WILD, MEXICANS CULTIVATED THE BUGS ON THEIR FARMS.

IT TAKES UP TO 70,000 DRIED-UP BUGS TO MAKE 454 GRAMS OR 1 POUND OF DYESTUFF.

BUT...JUST SO YOU KNOW

THE DYESTUFF DIDN'T LOOK LIKE A BUNCH OF DRIED BUGS. IT JUST LOOKED LIKE ITTY-BITTY GRAINY THINGIES.

EUROPE

IN 1519, THE FIRST SHIPMENT OF COCHINEAL DYESTUFF ARRIVED IN SPAIN.

THE COCHINEAL DYESTUFF CAUGHT ON IN **EUROPE**.

BY THE 1570s, SPAIN'S **COCHINEAL DYESTUFF** BUSINESS WAS **RED HOT.**

NO ONE HAS A CLUE HOW OUR DYESTUFF IS MADE.

THE **NEW RED** 10 TIMES MORE POWERFUL THAN ST. JOHN'S BLOOD ····· THE SAME AMOUNT MAKES 30 TIMES MORE DYE THAN ARMENIAN RED

ENVIOUS EUROPEANS

MWAHAHA, WE HAVE A WORLD MONOPOLY ON THIS DYESTUFF AND WE'RE MAKING A FORTUNE.

WE MUST GET OUR OWN COCHINEAL SUPPLY.

GRRR.

I WANT TO GET RICH TOO!

33

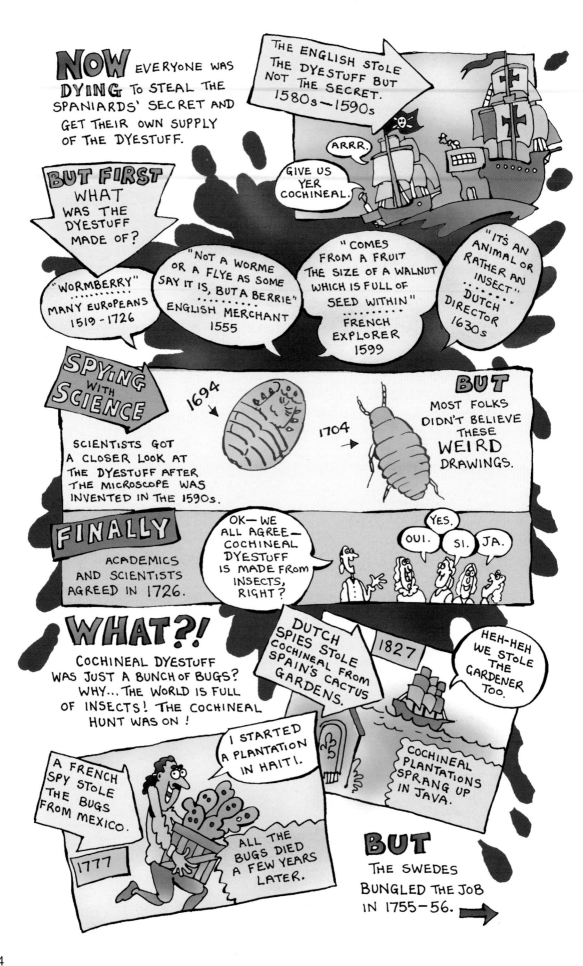

SWEDEN GETS THE SPY BUG

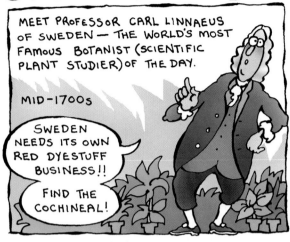

MEET PROFESSOR CARL LINNAEUS OF SWEDEN — THE WORLD'S MOST FAMOUS BOTANIST (SCIENTIFIC PLANT STUDIER) OF THE DAY.

MID-1700s

SWEDEN NEEDS ITS OWN RED DYESTUFF BUSINESS!!

FIND THE COCHINEAL!

THE FAMOUS PROFESSOR ENCOURAGED HIS STUDENTS TO TRAVEL THE GLOBE AND SEARCH OUT NEW SPECIES.

BRING ME BACK SPECIMENS.

MEXICO WAS OUT OF COURSE.

FORBIDDEN

NO ENTRY

CLEAR OFF

ONE OF THE PROFESSOR'S DISCIPLES — 30-YEAR-OLD DANIEL ROLANDER — SAILED TO SOUTH AMERICA'S SURINAM TO TRY HIS LUCK AT COCHINEAL SPYING.

SURINAM

MEXICO

WHERE... GRUNT... SWAT... OUCH... UG... TADAAA! ROLANDER FOUND WHAT HE WAS LOOKING FOR.

GASP!

HELLO

BUT COCHINEAL ARE NOTORIOUSLY BAD TRAVELERS.

I LIKE TO BE DRY

AND NOT TOO HOT OR TOO COLD.

AND I REFUSE TO BUDGE WITHOUT MY BELOVED CACTUS

...WHICH CAN ALSO BE A TEMPERAMENTAL TRAVELER.

SO ROLANDER CREATED A GLASS TERRARIUM FOR THE INSECTS AND THEIR CACTI.

THANK YOU.

This bug-boggled case of miscommunication killed off Professor Carl Linnaeus's hopes for Sweden's very own cochineal dyestuff business. The red with rage professor wrote "About *Coccionella* I do not wish to speak, never wish to think or remember." Daniel Rolander and the professor ended up hating each other, Rolander's career as a botanist went nowhere, and he faded into obscurity.

What about the insects? The spying continued. The bugs "escaped" from the Mexican border several times. By the 1830s, cochineal were breeding all over the place. But in 1856, the whole business changed when an 18-year-old Englishman, William Henry Perkin, mixed a bunch of chemicals and made mauve. The new age of synthetic dyes had begun.

The rainbow of beautiful man-made colors that we wear today have mostly replaced natural dyes. The cochineal business has never been the same.

RADIO BLAH-BLAH

What's that? It's morse code and it spells ... "Botch up."

It's World War II (1939 – 45) again, (you're becoming quite the expert on WWII espionage) and you're about to tune into one of the deadliest cat-and-mouse radio games of the war.

But first, a little background music. By the end of 1941, Nazi Germany and her allies had taken control of most of Europe (except for the neutral countries). Many ordinary men and women volunteered to become spies, placing themselves in awful danger when they sneaked into these enemy-occupied lands. They trained in the United Kingdom's secret spy organization the Special Operations Executive (yes, you read all about the SOE's spy schools in Chapter 1) for various specialized jobs.

One dead important SOE spy job was that of the radio operator. Communications were vitally important as the SOE not only needed to hear what was happening inside enemy territories, but they also needed to give instructions to the agents.

Which brings us to this next nasty story. The location is the enemy-occupied Netherlands, and a Dutch spy's radio is about to spell out a deadly message ...

SOMEONE IN THE RADIO ROOM ISN'T PAYING ATTENTION!

LONDON ENGLAND

GERMAN-OCCUPIED LAND 1941-42

THE NETHERLANDS

GERMANY

And so ended the SOE's biggest bungled spy campaign and Germany's most successful counter-espionage operation of the war.

But why, oh why, did London ignore those warning signals that were standard spy radio protocol? The SOE knew that stressed-out spies made morse code botches all the time. In fact, some transmissions were so bad, they were unreadable. London made the wrong judgment call here, and the consequences were awful. The entire Netherlands' operation fell into German hands. In 1942 – 43, some 50 SOE agents and hundreds of civilian helpers were killed. 12 aircraft were shot down during these spy deliveries and 18 SOE spy radios came under German control.

After the war, Giskes wrote all about his radio game with England in his book, *London Calling North Pole*.

ROGUE BROGUE

A soldier's accent starts a rumor, fools a spy, and ... uh-ohhh

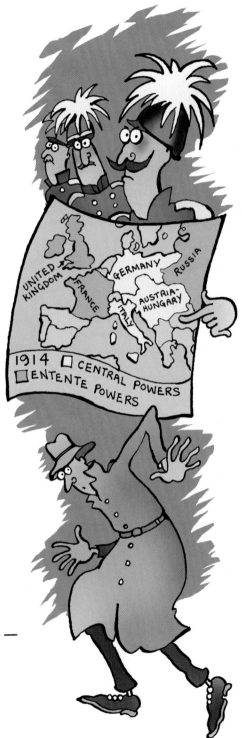

Gasp! Before World War I (1914 – 18) broke out, Europe was a tense and pushy place and spies were everywhere, sneakily trying to see what the neighbors were up to. Talk about competitive! Some countries vied for overseas trade and power, others for land, some got into a great naval arms race, and nearly all signed treaties with one another for power and protection. These treaties ended up dividing Europe into two camps: the Entente Powers and the Central Powers.

On June 28, 1914, when Austria's heir to the throne, Archduke Franz Ferdinand, got himself assassinated, things rapidly spun out of control ... and ... oh, you want details? OK ... Austria-Hungary blamed Serbia and declared war on them, then the Russians mobilized their troops, Germany then declared war on Russia and then France and then invaded Belgium, then ... OK, OK I'll stop. In a nutshell, all those secret treaties fired everyone up, all those European countries and their colonies throughout the world jumped in and World War I, one of the deadliest wars in human history, began.

But just hours before Great Britain declared war on Germany (August 4, 1914), Britain's spy-catching organization — the M05 — did something stunningly sneaky, which left Germany scrambling to find new agents. But uh-ohhh, one of their new spies made a huge error that landed Germany in the mud.

ACHH!
GERMAN SPIES WERE IN A DREADFUL PICKLE AT THE BEGINNING OF WORLD WAR I (1914), HERE'S HOW IT HAPPENED:

THE STORY STARTS ABOUT A DECADE BEFORE WWI WHEN READERS ALL OVER THE BRITISH ISLES WERE GOBBLING UP A NEW PUBLISHING PHENOMENON — SPY THRILLERS!! NEWSPAPERS GOT IN ON THE ACT TOO.

OVER 300 SPY NOVELS WERE PUBLISHED FROM 1901–1914

MOST OF THE BAD GUY SPIES WERE GERMANS.

ERSKINE CHILDERS THE RIDDLE OF THE SANDS 1903

WILLIAM LE QUEUX SPIES OF THE KAISER 1909

DO YOU VANT ZE SAME HAIRCUT?

THE KAISER'S SPIES COULD BE ANYONE INCLUDING YOUR BARBER.

SOON, SPY-FEVERED BRITS SQUINTED DISTRUSTFULLY OVER THE TOPS OF THEIR READING GLASSES AT INNOCENT GERMANS EVERYWHERE.

ARGHH!

POLICE STATIONS AROUND BRITAIN WERE FLOODED WITH REPORTS ABOUT GERMAN SPIES.

BRITAIN WAS ALARMED SO THE SECRET SERVICE BUREAU WAS CREATED IN 1909 WITH 19 MILITARY INTELLIGENCE UNITS. MO5 WAS THE SPY-CATCHING UNIT.

THIS TURNED OUT TO BE A RIPPING GOOD IDEA BECAUSE OVER TIME, THE MO5 IDENTIFIED EVERY GERMAN SPY IN BRITAIN.

LET'S ARREST THEM.

NO WAIT. IF WE ARREST THESE SPIES NOW, GERMANY WILL SEND NEW ONES AND IT WILL TAKE TIME FOR US TO FIND THEM.

THEN UH-OHHH...
WAR!
MO5 WAS SECRETLY GIVEN 12 HOURS' NOTICE THAT BRITAIN WAS ABOUT TO DECLARE WAR ON GERMANY.

OK. NOW IT'S TIME TO ARREST THOSE 22 SPIES.

SEND THESE PRE-ARRANGED ENCODED TELEGRAMS TO THE POLICE AROUND THE COUNTRY.

If only Lody had reworded his telegram. From General von Moltke's point of view, there's a huge difference between "I have been informed" and "I heard a rumor." Some say that Lody's misinformation (false information) and miscommunication (not communicating clearly) cost Germany the war. After the German defeat at the Battle of the Marne, both sides dug in and spent the rest of the war mired in mud and trench warfare on Europe's Western Front.

Lody was arrested in October, put on trial, and convicted. It was plastered all over the newspapers, of course. Lody's patriotism and honor, revealed during the trial, drew the admiration of both the British and German public. On November 6, 1914, Lody became the the first person to be executed at the Tower of London in over 150 years and the first foreign spy to be executed in WWI.

The German navy named a destroyer, the *Hans Lody,* after this WWI spy in 1935.

CHAPTER 3
IT SEEMED LIKE A
GOOD IDEA
AT THE TIME.

Spying is so darned difficult!
Doesn't matter if your espionage goal
is simple or super-complex, when you
plan your mission, you must often
be bold and daring, clever, and creative!
You must always be willing to consider
new ideas to get the spy job done.

But beware. Some of your good ideas,
clever schemes, and innovative plots
may miss the mark and backfire big
time. What happens then? You have
a big fat fizzled spy failure on your
hands — and that's never good news.

ASININE ASSASSINATION
HEADS UP FOR AN ANCIENT CHINESE BOTCH-UP

ACOUSTIC KITTY
COOL CONCEPT? ... OR A PURRFECTLY BAD IDEA?

DELAYED DECRYPTION
ARAB'S PLODDING PLOT FIZZLES

GROSS MISCOMMUNICATION
A SICK LITTLE STRATEGY FROM 1796

FUNNY MONEY
A PRICELESS END TO A GREEDY SCHEME

ASININE ASSASSINATION

Warning! This spy plot is a killer.

Killing an ancient Chinese king. That's what this plot is all about. Mwaahahaaa! (Evil laugh.)

Now this old king lived way, way back in ancient history when China was divided into loads of small feudal lands. These were lands (called fiefs) that a king allowed his nobles (called vassals) to control. In return, the nobles pledged their loyalty, money, and provided military services whenever the king asked.

This system of government trickled down to the peasants too: they were allowed to farm a strip of land in return for paying a tax and promising to fight when asked. After centuries of these feudal lands clobbering and absorbing one another, 7 big states or kingdoms emerged. Did the fighting stop then? Of course not! These kingdoms kept at it from 475 BCE to 221 BCE during a time that the historians call the Warring States Period.

Then the year 227 BCE arrived. And it looked like the winner would be the Kingdom of Qin. Qin's king had a huge army! He'd subdued the states of Han and Zhao. Now he set his sights on the land of Yan, which got the Prince of Yan dead worried. His army was much weaker you see.

So how could the king of Qin be stopped? The Crown Prince of Yan needed a good idea. Fast!

WAHHHH!

THE KING RAN AROUND A PILLAR WHILE EVERYONE STOOD AND STARED.

NO ONE NEAR THE KING WAS ALLOWED TO CARRY WEAPONS.

THE PALACE GUARDS DOWN THE HALL WERE ARMED, BUT THEY WEREN'T ALLOWED TO APPROACH THE KING UNLESS THEY WERE CALLED.

KAPOW!

THE WEAPONLESS KING PUNCHED JING KE...

BAM!

THE KING'S DOCTOR SWUNG HIS MEDICINE BAG...

OUCH!

FINALLY, THE KING FREED HIS SWORD AND SLASHED JING KE'S THIGH.

MISSED

JING KE THREW THE DAGGER AT THE KING.

OUCH OUCH!

SURPRISE SURPRISE! THE PLOT FAILED.

THEN JING KE MET HIS END!! THE KING SLASHED HIM EIGHT TIMES AND THE PALACE GUARDS FINALLY CAME AND FINISHED HIM OFF.

THEN GRRR!

I'M SO ANGRY! GO TELL MY ARMY TO INVADE YAN.

AFTER THE ASSASSINATION BOTCH-UP, THE KING OF QIN TOOK CONTROL OF YAN.

THE KING OF YAN WAS FORCED TO KILL HIS SON, PRINCE TAN, TO KEEP THE PEACE WITH THE KING OF QIN.

The assassination idea was a dead loss. Prince Tan and Jing Ke failed to kill Qin's king, failed to stop him from taking over Yan, and they got themselves killed too. Within five years, the king of Qin subdued the last few kingdoms and, in 221 BCE, created a country that has remained unified to this very day. The king of Qin became Qin Shi Huang, which means First Emperor of the Qin dynasty. He died in 210 BCE.

Qin Shi Huang's tomb was discovered by a farmer in 1974. It contains a life-sized terracotta army of over 8,000 soldiers, 670 horses, 130 chariots, and more.

51

DELAYED DECRYPTION

Can a secret message topple the Sultan?

Oh fiddle-faddle. In the year 1600, an Arab spy stole a secret message that was sure to prove that the Sultan of Morocco was up to no good. Trouble was, the message was all fudged up. It was written in code. What was the sultan up to? Proposing secret deals with European Christians — that's what.

Now back in the 1500s and 1600s, there was mistrust everywhere, and a lot of it had to do with religion. The Muslims of the Arab world were still miffed after the Christians came down and fought a series of religious wars against them called the Crusades (1095 – 1272). Getting kicked out of Spain more recently didn't help either. The European Christians were squabbling among themselves too. Two branches of the Christian religion — the Catholics and the Protestants — annoyed each other big time.

Then just to keep things interesting, the Ottoman empire entered the picture too. This huge empire that was governed by the Muslim Turks from 1299 to 1923 (yes, the same folks from present-day Turkey) were tussling with Spain over control of the Mediterranean Sea routes. The Ottomans had control of many trade routes, but Spain with its growing sea power and wealth wanted in on the money-making action.

The sultan of Morocco, who was sitting on a prime piece of strategically located land (see the map), bent these rivalries to his own advantage, proposing alliances as he tried to devise ways to get richer and more powerful. But the spy was hot on his trail. . .

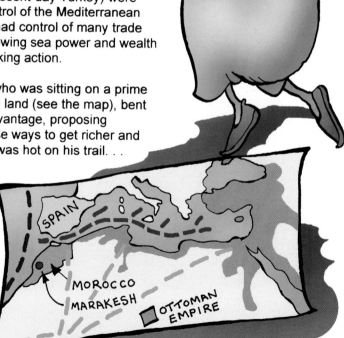

TRADE ROUTES:
- - - MEDITERRANEAN
- - ATLANTIC OCEAN - - -
- - - SAHARA DESERT - - -

Pah! The spy clearly never read those dusty old Arab How to Crack Codes books. Though it seemed like a good idea at the time, the spy took far too long to decode the message.

As for Sultan Ahmad al-Mansur, though he started his rule with a bang after his stunning victory at Alcazar, his masterful international wheeling and dealing couldn't save him from the age-old problem of simply spending too much. By 1603, when Sultan Ahmad al-Mansur died of the plague in, the huge costs of running a big army, building a pricey palace, plus the expense of maintaining control of his conquest in Western Sudan, had taken the shine off this great man's ambitions. And, no, he never became a caliph.

William Shakespeare, who lived during the same time, modeled his Prince of Morocco after the sultan in *The Merchant of Venice* — the play that has the famous line "All that glitters is not gold."

GROSS MISCOMMUNICATION

**A gutsy spy trick
that's hard to swallow.**

Warning: This next spy ploy is sick, sick, sick! Though it seemed like a good idea at the time, the ending really stank. What a mess!

But before you chew up the cartoons, taste a little slice of history first. From 1789 to 1799, France was in a froth. Lower- and middleclass French people had given their king and queen the old heave-ho and had sliced off their heads with a guillotine in 1793. French nobles fled to other countries to escape the same fate.

During this upheaval, called the French Revolution, ordinary folk strived for what we take for granted today. The rights of equality and freedom for everyone, the universal rights to education and to own land, etc. France's feudal system really sucked if you weren't a noble. (It sucked just as much for peasants back in old China's feudal system too. See "Asinine Assassination.") Poor French people were considered to to be the property of the rich and weren't allowed to hunt for a little meat or even own a pigeon!

But the rest of Europe with their kings, queens, and nobles firmly in place were not thrilled about the recent events in France. They banded together and formed the first of 7 coalitions to invade France and put the troublemakers back in their places. But thanks to a brilliant army leader called Napoleon Bonaparte, the French army not only fought off the invading European armies but carried on battling beyond France's borders.

Ready for the sick little spy story now? Hold onto your guts and read on.

WHAT A BELLYACHE!

SLICE

WHAT A HEADACHE!

GUILLOTINE

EUROPE 1797

AUSTRIAN MONARCHY

FRANCE

SPY JOB FOUL-UP HERE

WHAT A MESS!

Ewwww. What seemed like a good idea at the time turned out to be a big bellyache for Austria. Thanks to the wax-ball message that spewed out of the spy's stomach, Napoleon knew that the Austrians were coming. He moved the French troops to the north to wait and prepare for battle.

Napoleon's 23,000 soldiers defeated Alvinzi's 28,000 Austrians at the Battle of Rivoli on January 14 – 15, 1797, and Field Marshal Dagobert von Wurmser was forced to surrender the fort at Mantua a few weeks later. This huge victory for France led to the French occupation of northern Italy.

Two years later, Napoleon became the leader of France.

OK, to be fair, the ancient Chinese did the same weird wax-ball swallowing trick too, but their spy messages were written on silk.

FUNNY MONEY

This plot is priceless!

What a laugh! (For us, not the spy, of course.) One day, an ambassador's sly servant had a great idea. He'd get rich quick by becoming a spy. He knew that his boss's valuable secrets were worth a fortune to the right people.

The spy was living in a city swarming with spies. During World War II, three cities were spy magnets: Bern in Switzerland, Lisbon in Portugal, and our spy's city, Ankara in Turkey. These cities were neutral in 1943 – 44, when this story took place (Turkey joined the war in 1945). So foreign governments from both sides of the conflict had set up their embassies there. An embassy is a fancy building that contains an important diplomat or ambassador (someone who represents his or her country) as well as a bunch of staff to run it.

With so many embassies in these cities, it wasn't uncommon for diplomats of enemy countries to attend the same social gatherings and even to make polite small talk with one another. With so many hush-hush embassy meetings, confidential conversations, and secret reports to overhear or intercept, these three cities were stuffed full of intrigue and espionage.

All set for a tricky, true tale of spies, secrets, money, and greed? Oh goody.

MY "GET RICH QUICK" IDEA IS WORKING!

WORLD WAR II

NEUTRAL COUNTRIES IN 1943-44

LISBON
PORTUGAL
BERN
SWITZERLAND
EUROPE
TURKEY
ASIA
ANKARA

Bazna was a successful spy — it's true, but Bazna spied to make money plain and simple. His "get rich quick" scheme, which seemed like a good idea at the time, ended in a big fizzle. He lost his job, his money, and his career. Bazna could never be trusted to work in embassies ever again. What a priceless payoff for a greedy spy!

After the war, Bazna's German Embassy contact man, L.C. Moyzisch, wrote a best-selling book called *Operation Cicero* and made a fortune. Then a movie about Cicero called *5 Fingers* made even more money. Bazna wrote a book called *I Was Cicero*, but it wasn't nearly as successful. Bazna died a poor man in 1970.

ACOUSTIC KITTY

**Cold War spies?
What were they thinking?**

But back in the early 1960s, the United States of America were willing to try just about ANYTHING to get inside information about their enemy — the Soviet Union. (The Soviets were just as bad.)

Yes, you guessed it — it's the Cold War again (1945 – 91), that chilling era when these two competitive superpowers turned to the skills of their scientists and engineers to develop and build nuclear weapons of mass destruction. This made folks as nervous as long-tailed cats in a room full of rocking chairs, especially when the USA's close neighbor Cuba (just 145 kilometers, or 90 miles, away) started building missile bases with the help of their friends, the Soviet Union. Take a guess about where those missiles were going to point.

With a sense of urgency, the USA's spy network, the CIA, explored every way to snoop on the Soviets. The CIA also turned to their scientists at the Directorate of Science and Technology for fresh, innovative ideas like the stunner in this next story.

HERE'S A THOUGHT. LET'S USE CATS TO SPY ON THE SOVIETS.

GOOD IDEA.

...USA...EARLY 1960s

MIAOW.

WHOSE BOMBS ARE BIGGER?

SOVIET UNION

USA

CUBA

NUCLEAR FISION— WHAT A BLAST!

UH-OHHH... THIS DOESN'T LOOK GOOD.

CAREFUL NOW. WE DON'T WANT TO SET OFF A CHAIN REACTION.

GO SEE WHAT THEY'RE DOING NOW.

☐ USA
☐ THE USA's ALLIES
☐ SOVIET UNION
☐ SOVIET ALLIES

Relax. The Cuban Missile Crisis got sorted out in 1962.

EARLY 1960s: AMERICA'S INTELLIGENCE ORGANIZATION, THE **CIA**, WAS DESPERATE TO GET ANY SOVIET INTELLIGENCE.

SHUSHH, COMRADE. SOMVON'S BEHIND ZAT TREE.

GET ANY INFORMATION?

NOPE.

SPIES ARE USELESS IN CERTAIN SITUATIONS. WHAT WE REALLY NEED IS A MOBILE BUGGING DEVICE

THAT DOESN'T LOOK SUSPICIOUS.

SO THE **CIA** ASKED THE WIZARDS (ENGINEERS AND SCIENTISTS) AT THE **DIRECTORATE** OF **SCIENCE** AND **TECHNOLOGY** TO COME UP WITH SOMETHING CLEVER.

SURE NO PROBLEM.

FINALLY SOME BRIGHT SPARK CAME UP WITH A **PURRFECT PLAN**.

WHY NOT HIDE THE BUGGING DEVICE ON SPECIALLY TRAINED KITTY CATS?!?

GO FOR IT! HERE'S A FEW MILLION $$$ TO START YOUR RESEARCH.

AND SO THE TOP-SECRET PROJECT ACOUSTIC KITTY WAS BORN.

OK, have you sensitive types finished groaning and the rest of you finished laughing?

Right then ... Let's conclude this fine sample of espionage failure.

In 1967, Project Acoustic Kitty was scratched. Though the scientists were praised, a censored CIA memo (released under *the Freedom of Information Act*) concluded: *"Our final examination of trained cats [deleted] for [deleted] use in the [deleted] convinced us that the program would not lend itself in a practical sense to our highly specialized needs."*

Just a fancy way of saying that the whole undertaking was a [deleted] failure. The total cost of Project Acoustic Kitty was estimated to be over $15 million.

CHAPTER 4
HOW HARD COULD IT BE ?

Here's a warning for all you ultra-powerful, super-successful, or just plain proud people out there. It may be easy to think that you can get away with anything, but you can't. When it comes to the sneaky, sly world of spying, beware!

Never forget that in the arena of espionage, you can never be too humble. If you forget that others can be just as intelligent, sneaky, or as sharp as you (and maybe even more so), you may be in for a terrible tumble.

So think twice before you say "How hard can it be?" Got that? Good.

LISTLESS LEADER

MIGHTY OLD POOP BLOWS IT

MATA HARI

FAMOUS WOMAN'S DOWNFALL

NUCLEAR EGO

BOOM KABOOM

BOMB PLOT BLOWS UP IN FRANCE'S FACE

LISTLESS LEADER

An emperor mucks up.

Crap! (Am I allowed to say this word? Yes, I am. The publisher didn't delete it.) An emperor from the 8th century called Constantine Kopronymos (Kopronymos is a Greek word that means "name of dung.") was about to get his spies into deep doo-doo. All because he thought "How hard could it be?" when his enemy made a secret proposal.

This old poop ruled the Byzantine empire from 741 to 775. You know about the Byzantine empire right? In the late 3rd century, the Roman empire split in half. One emperor ruled from Italy, the other from Greece. Then in the 4th century, a fellow called Constantine the Great became the sole emperor of the whole lot. (Mr. "the Great" was the first of 11 Constantines; our man Kopronymos was number 5.)

Constantine the Great moved the empire's capital to an old Greek colony called Byzantium and renamed it Nova Roma (New Rome). But that name didn't stick, everyone called the place Constantinople (Constantine's City) instead. For over a thousand years after that, the Byzantine empire was a force to be reckoned with.

Now, back to the old poop — Constantine Kopronymos. If you're interested in knowing how this emperor got his foul name, and how he mucked up his espionage team, read on.

BUT
CONSTANTINE DIDN'T SPEND ALL HIS TIME DESTROYING RELIGIOUS ICONS AND GETTING MEAN WITH THE MONKS.
OUCH. OUCH.
I'M A BRILLIANT GENERAL TOO.
ANY NEW SPY NEWS? I NEED TO PLAN MY NEXT MILITARY MOVE.
LIST
NEXT ON THE LIST: CONSTANTINE FOUGHT WITH THE ARABS. A TRUCE WAS DECLARED.
WHAT'S NEXT?
LIST
WE BYZANTINES HAVE BEEN TRYING TO CONTROL THOSE BLASTED BULGARS FOR YEARS!
BLACK SEA
BULGARS
CONSTANTINOPLE
BYZANTINES
THE BULGARS! ATTACK!
THE BULGARS MIGRATED TO EUROPE FROM CENTRAL ASIA IN THE 5TH CENTURY.
CONSTANTINE WAGED 9 MILITARY CAMPAIGNS AGAINST THE BULGARS FROM 756 TO 775.
YARGH!
RAAAGH!
SOMETIMES THE BYZANTINES WON, SOMETIMES THE BULGARS WON.
I WISH MY SPIES COULD HAVE PREDICTED THAT NASTY STORM.
IN 774 CONSTANTINE'S SHIPS GOT WRECKED
WHILE CARRYING THOUSANDS OF SOLDIERS TO FIGHT THE BULGARS.
BUT
WAR WITH THE BYZANTINES CAUSED MAJOR LEADERSHIP PROBLEMS WITH THE BULGARS.
YOU LOST US ANOTHER BATTLE? NEXT!
THE BULGARS HAD 7 KHANS (RULERS) WITHIN 15 YEARS.
EX-KHAN
IN 775, THE BULGARS' NEW KHAN, TELERIG, WAS GETTING WORRIED.
IF I DON'T DO WELL IN BATTLE, I'LL PROBABLY BE KILLED BY MY OWN PEOPLE, JUST LIKE THE LAST KHAN.

In 775, Emperor Constantine Kopronymos learned the hard way never to underestimate the enemy. He died the same year. (No, not of embarrassment silly — of natural causes.)

Constantine was buried with the other emperors in Constantinople's Church of the Holy Apostles. But the old poop was so hated because of his religious icon-smashing and meanness to monks that his bones were dug up in the 9th century and chucked into the sea.

The Byzantines and the Bulgars battled on and off for another several hundred years until the Ottoman empire beat them both in the 15th century.

MATA HARI

Sexpionage! Er … I mean espionage!

Ask anyone to list the world's most famous female spies. Go on, I dare you. Just be sure to emphasize the word FAMOUS. What name springs to everyone's lips and often tops the list? Mata Hari. No book about spy failures would be complete without her.

Mata Hari was an entertainment star long before World War I broke out in 1914. While Europe had its serious side in the decade leading up to the war, (politics, power struggles, battleship building, and whatnot), it also had a fun, frivolous, and cultural side. In the decade before the war, Europeans were intrigued by the new art form — modern dance — and went gaga over anything Asian. Mata Hari combined the two interests and danced in a style unique to European theatergoers. And … er … oh yeah … her dances were sizzlingly scandalous and super-sexy too.

When World War I broke out, Mata Hari decided to use her sexy talents to spy. After all, how hard could it be?

MATA HARI
1876—1917

HOW DID SHE GET SO FAMOUS?

DUTCH BORN MARGARETHA ZELLE LEFT A BAD MARRIAGE IN 1904 - - -

ONLY TO DISCOVER - -

WAIT A MINUTE... I HAVE **NO** MONEY!!

SO SHE TOOK A CHANCE AND WENT TO PARIS, FRANCE.

1905

I'LL FIND WORK HERE. HOW HARD CAN IT BE?

SOME OF HER MARRIED LIFE WAS SPENT IN JAVA, MALAYSIA.

IN PARIS, MARGARETHA BORROWED SOME EXOTIC COSTUMES FROM AN ORIENTAL ARTS MUSEUM AND LIED!

I'LL PRETEND TO BE A PRINCESS FROM JAVA.

SHE GAVE HERSELF THE STAGE NAME MATA HARI AND THEN SHE DANCED.

I'LL SAY I WAS TRAINED AS A HINDU TEMPLE DANCER.

MATA HARI WAS AN OVERNIGHT SUCCESS! EUROPE HAD NEVER SEEN SUCH EXOTIC, SEXY DANCES BEFORE. SHE WOWED AND SCANDALIZED AUDIENCES WHEREVER SHE DANCED.

GASP!

OH MY!

SEND FOR A DOCTOR! HENRI IS HAVING A HEART ATTACK!

I COPIED THE DANCE STYLE THAT I SAW IN JAVA, BUT I ADDED MY OWN NAUGHTY MOVES.

PARIS

WOW

MATA HARI TOOK OFF MOST OF HER CLOTHES WHEN SHE DANCED. NEAR-NUDITY ON THE STAGE WAS VERY RARE BACK IN 1905.

VIENNA

MADRID

WOW

BERLIN

WIGGLE

Spying! How hard could it be? Mata Hari paid a deadly price for not taking espionage seriously enough.

During her two-day trial in Paris, the French said that they never hired Mata Hari to spy for them. Did Mata Hari lie? Did the French lie? We may never know. The espionage world is so darned murky. And speaking of murky, why did the Germans send a radio message about Mata Hari and her spy name, H-21, in a radio code that they knew had been broken by the British and the French?

But whether or not Mata Hari was a single agent, a double agent working for two countries, or just a woman pretending to spy to make some extra money, the name Mata Hari has come to mean a sneaky and seductive, if not successful, female spy.

NUCLEAR EGO

This spy plot bombs!

BLAST! And I mean it! In the decades after World War II, the nuclear age expanded across the globe. France grew more and more concerned about its reputation. The country wanted to be a nuclear power, but it didn't want to be caught wrecking the environment. All it needed was a foolproof plan to prevent a public relations bombshell. How hard could it be?

Now, folks have always been dead twitchy about weapons of mass destruction. Scientists too. Let's face it, the radiation from nuclear bombs and nuclear testing can be a real killer and have an awful impact on the environment. Very few countries have developed their own nuclear weapons (today you can count them on 2 hands), but when France became the 4th nation to make and test nuclear weapons back in 1960, it soon got itself into hot water with the general public.

While the USA, the Soviet Union, and China tested their weapons and collected data in remote spots within their borders (the USA shared its data with the United Kingdom), France, on the other hand, conducted 193 of its 210 tests far from home on the Mururoa Atoll in French Polynesia.

Talk about an unpopular move! From the early 1960s onwards, France was swamped with complaints and protests from environmental groups, peace groups, and governments too. And things got really nasty when the protesters started showing up at its Pacific Ocean test site.

In 1985, France's secret service found out that the environmental watchdog group, *Greenpeace,* would be interrupting its next round of tests. Something had to be done.

THEN ON **JULY 10**
AN HOUR OR SO BEFORE MIDNIGHT...

A DIVER SILENTLY SLIPPED INTO THE WATER AND SWAM TOWARD AUCKLAND'S MARSDEN WHARF — WHERE THE PROTEST SHIP THE *RAINBOW WARRIOR* WAS DOCKED.

QUIET PLOP

HE CARRIED TWO LIMPET MINES THAT HAD BEEN SMUGGLED INTO NEW ZEALAND ABOARD THE YACHT *OUVEA*.

EXPLOSIVES INSIDE
SLIMY LIMPET GOO INSIDE
BOTH STICK LIKE GLUE

A LIMPET MINE IS AN UNDERWATER EXPLOSIVE THAT ATTACHES TO A SHIP'S METAL HULL WITH MAGNETS. IT'S NAMED AFTER THE LIMPET — A CLINGY LITTLE MOLLUSK.

THE DIVER ATTACHED TWO MINES TO THE *RAINBOW WARRIOR'S* HULL AND THE PROPELLER'S SHAFT.

TICK TICK

JOB DONE!

THE TIMERS WERE SET TO BLOW 10 MINUTES APART — JUST BEFORE MIDNIGHT.

THE DIVER CLIMBED BACK INTO THE INFLATABLE DINGHY AND MOTORED TOWARD A PRE-ARRANGED SPOT — WHERE HE TIED UP THE DINGHY AND CLIMBED INTO THE "SWISS HONEYMOONERS'" RENTED VAN.

THE INFLATABLE DINGHY WAS ABANDONED. IT NEEDED TO BE UNTRACEABLE, SO IT HAD BEEN PURCHASED IN ENGLAND WITH CASH BY AN AGENT WHO GAVE A FALSE NAME AT HIS HOTEL.

EXIT PLANS
- THE CHARTERED YACHT SAILED AWAY IMMEDIATELY.
- THE TEAMS THAT FLEW IN INTENDED TO FLY OUT IN A FEW WEEKS' TIME — AFTER ALL THE FUSS HAD DIED DOWN.

THE POLICE HAD NO OTHER EVIDENCE AGAINST THE "SWISS COUPLE." THEY WERE JUST FOLLOWING ANY AND ALL LEADS.

THE SPIES STUCK TO THEIR COVER STORY.

BUT THEN THE SPY PLOT STARTED TO UNRAVEL WHEN THE POLICE ASKED COMMANDER MAFART THIS...

IF YOU'RE ON YOUR HONEYMOON, WHY ARE YOU KEEPING A TALLY OF YOUR TRIP'S EXPENSES?

ER... ER... FORCE OF HABIT.

BUT WHY ARE YOU "PADDING" OR ADDING EXTRA FALSE AMOUNTS TO YOUR EXPENSE LIST?

.....

YOU WOULD ONLY DO THAT IF YOU WANTED TO GET EXTRA MONEY FROM YOUR BOSS WHEN HE OR SHE REPAYS YOU.

AFTER THE QUESTIONING, COMMANDER MAFART QUICKLY MADE A PHONE CALL. THE NEW ZEALAND POLICE TRACED IT TO AN UNLISTED NUMBER IN FRANCE.

BUT WHEN THE NEW ZEALAND POLICE ASKED FRANCE'S SECRET SERVICE (DGSE) TO GIVE THEM THE UNLISTED NUMBER...

THAT NUMBER DOES NOT EXIST.

THE NEW ZEALAND POLICE **IMMEDIATELY** KNEW THAT THE FRENCH WERE COVERING UP!! THE PHONE NUMBER HAD TO BE FROM SOME SECRET BRANCH OF FRANCE'S GOVERNMENT.

WHAT HAPPENED NEXT?

FRENCH SPIES CONFESS!

HUGE SCANDAL!

...AND ROTTEN PUBLICITY FOR THE FRENCH GOVERNMENT

Sinking a ship to stop bad publicity — how hard could it be? France found out how hard when they accidentally killed a man and then had their spy plot uncovered. The whole explosive mess was a public relations disaster and a diplomatic nightmare!

New Zealand was mad as blazes with France. Committing sabotage in a foreign country is a big no-no. Greenpeace was outraged too and so was the family of the *Rainbow Warrior*'s drowned crew member. France was fined big time and had to pay out $7 million (US) to New Zealand, over $8 million (US) to Greenpeace plus a huge amount to the family of the *Rainbow Warrior's* dead crew member. It took years to normalize relations between New Zealand and France.

Only two agents were caught and arrested; the "honeymooners'" support team. The French military spies, Commander Alain Mafart and Captain Dominique Prieur, were both sentenced to 10 years in prison, but after a deal, which put them into the custody of the French military, both were released much sooner.

The nuclear tests that Greenpeace wanted to protest took place in the end.

CHAPTER **5**

ON SECOND THOUGHT...

Hey, all you spy chiefs, captains
of industry, military commanders,
and leaders of the land!
You pay someone to work for you
and you expect loyalty, honesty,
and a job well done. Right? But
here's a shocker. Someone you
trust might not give a rat's whisker
about you or your secret plans
and information. Gasp!

ARGHHHH!

A valued spy or employee
could very well be a double-dealing
double-crosser who is selling
you out for a price.

So beware! The person
who you least suspect may
have had second thoughts
and might now be your enemy,
your betrayer.

DAM
TRAITOR

ANCIENT
CHINESE
CHEAT

WHACK
A MOLE

SELLING OUT
TO THE SOVIETS

THE
PERSUADED
PERSIAN

TATTLED ON
AND LIED TO

THE
FAMILY
PLOT

SWINDLING
COMPANY
SNEAK

DAM TRAITOR

Double-dealer's swampy scheme

Dam! No, I'm not swearing. I'm talking about unplugging a dammed river and how a darned devious, double-dealing spy did it. Dang it!

This plot played out well over 2,000 years ago during ancient China's longest running kingship — the Zhou dynasty (1045-ish – 256 BCE). The Zhous had muscled out their rotten neighbors — the corrupt old Shang Dynasty — around 1045 and now ruled a huge land mass. But the land was far too big for one little old king to rule. (There were really bad communications and roads back then.) So lords were appointed to oversee smaller states just as long as they agreed to support the king. (Yep, it's the feudal system all right.) But in 771 BCE, barbarians invaded Western Zhou and beheaded the king. Ouch! The prince fled to Eastern Zhou and ruled from there. But from now on, all Zhou kings had few powers over their lords. Some lords even created their own independent kingdoms. And, oh yeah, Eastern and Western Zhou were never the best of friends either.

During the Zhou dynasty, Chinese technology and culture took amazing strides forward. Advances were made in the military, the field of philosophy, and iron working (making things like amazing bronze pots). And don't forget about their dams and irrigation (crop-watering) canals.

Now, back to the dam spy plot. In 300 BCE, ancient China was smack in the middle of a long, gruesome war called the Warring States Period (475 – 221 BCE) — a power struggle between Zhou's vassal lords and its offshoot kingdoms. Always keen to nettle his enemy, a ruler of Western Zhou was delighted when a clever spy proposed a brilliant scheme that was sure to irrigate, I mean irritate, Eastern Zhou.

I HAVE A DAM PLAN TO MAKE MONEY.

ZHOU, 300 BCE

N
WEST — EAST
S

Betrayed! The ruler of Western Zhou failed to dry up his neighbor's economy thanks to that double-crossing Su-Tzu. Eastern Zhou's ruler never caught on that Su-Tzu was double-dealing and making twice the money on one mission. The ruler was far too happy that his river was no longer blocked. His farmers grew a bumper rice crop that season.

In 221 BCE, all the dam warfare between the Zhous came to an end after a fellow called Qin marched in and took control of both regions.

Spying, sabotaging, arguing, and negotiating over water rights is nothing new in Earth's history. After all, we're talking about an incredibly precious resource—fresh water.

THE PERSUADED PERSIAN

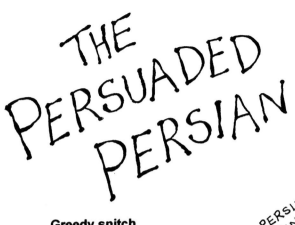

**Greedy snitch
switches sides.**

Yarghhh! (Blood-curdling war cry.) Will an ancient battle be botched by a snitching spys' lies?

Long, long ago, two neighboring superpowers who dominated Eastern Europe and Western Asia couldn't get along with each other at all. The Persians and the Romans had been playing tug-of-war with their shared border ever since the Romans had tried and failed to conquer Persia back in 92 BCE. Historians call their ongoing conflicts — wait for this catchy title — the *Roman-Persian Wars*. These enemies had been at it for so long that by the time this spy story took place around 530 BCE, the Roman empire was now called the Byzantine empire (that's right, you just read all about this in the Intro for "Listless Leader" on page 71). The Persian empire had changed too. Its first lot of leaders, the fair-minded Parthian dynasty, had been shoved out by the more intolerant Sassanid dynasty.

Now back to the ancient plot. Yarghhhh! (Another blood-curdling war cry.) A Persian spy had second thoughts about where his loyalties lay and caused major problems for a Sassanid king. Arghhh! (Cry of frustration.)

BYZANTINE EMPEROR

PERSIA'S KING

ARGHHHH!

SNITCHY SPY

530 BCE □ SASSANID EMPIRE AND VASSAL STATES   ■ BYZANTINE EMPIRE

TUG-OF-WAR

IT'S A GOOD JOB THAT OLD KING KAVADH WASN'T A MASSAGETAE. THESE NOMADS WHO FOLLOWED THEIR GRAZING HERDS OF CATTLE USED TO SACRIFICE THEIR OLD PEOPLE TO THEIR GOD, THE SUN, THEN THEY BOILED THEM AND ATE THEM. ...AND, OH YES... THE MASSAGETAE WERE GREAT FIGHTERS. THEIR FAVORITE WEAPON WAS THE BATTLE-AX.

BY THE TIME THAT THE PERSIAN SASSANIDS AND THE MASSAGETAE HAD REGROUPED TO ATTACK DARA, THE BYZANTINES HAD BOUGHT IN EXTRA SOLDIERS TO DEFEND IT. THE BUSY BYZANTINES EVEN HAD TIME TO DIG DEFENSE DITCHES TO HINDER THE ENEMY'S HORSES.

YARGHHHH!

BARGHHHH!

THE BYZANTINES WERE STILL OUTNUMBERED, BUT THOSE EXTRA TROOPS AND THE DITCH DIGGING DID THE TRICK. THEY WON THE BATTLE OF DARA.

BETTER LUCK NEXT TIME!

ARGHHHH!

THERE'S NO WORD WHERE THE SPY RETIRED WITH HIS RICHES.

Arghhh! (Cry of frustration.) King Kavadh was so upset! His spy's betrayal had tipped off the Byzantines and surely caused him to lose the conquest of Dara. One year later in 531, King Kadavh died of old age and maybe outrage too.

Dara was fought over time and time again, and exchanged hands a few times. The Roman-Persian Wars carried on and on, but neither side could maintain long campaigns far from their shared border. They just didn't have enough military resources to defend what they took. Would these tug-of-wars never end?

Shortly after their latest war ended in 628, Arab tribes, who had recently united under the religious banner of Islam, put a stop to the lot when they invaded the Persian empire and many Byzantine lands. And so ended 7 centuries of war between the Romans and the Persians.

THE FAMILY PLOT

Bamboozling big brother and big business.

Talk about big business, check out the pink on the map. In the early 1800s, all these lands were ruled by the British East India Company. And, oh my, this company certainly needed spies.

The company hatched in 1600 when the queen of England said to a group of businessmen: OK, you will be the only folks who can sell Asian goods in Britain. Now that's a monopoly! (A monopoly means one company has no competition for what it sells.) The traders moved to India, purchased Indian woven cotton cloth, then sold it to the West, where there was a huge demand for durable textiles for clothing. They bought and sold lots of other goods too, and they made a fortune!

But how did the trading company end up ruling so much of India? In the 1770s, India's old ruling Mughal empire had waned. Now India was no longer unified under one powerful banner but was divided into a collection of smaller states. The big rich trading company, with its English crown connections as well as its own army, signed treaties, trade and military agreements with the less powerful but ambitious individual leaders, and pretty soon the British East India Company ended up calling the shots and controlling the lot.

But most locals in India weren't exactly thrilled by their foreign controllers. The company knew this and fretted about secret schemes to topple them. Spies were hired to find out what was happening, but one sneaky plot shocked the British big time. They were being betrayed!

TRUST ME.

BRITISH EAST INDIA COMPANY

LAND CONTROLLED BY THE COMPANY IN: ■ 1765 ☐ 1837

INFORMANT'S INFO. CAME TO THE COMPANY OFFICES SUCH AS THE ONE HERE IN LUCKNOW.

LUCKNOW

THE COMPANY DIRECTOR AND HIS CHIEF MUNSHI, MAHOMED BAKER ALI, ANALYZED THE REPORTS.

WHAT'S YOUR OPINION?

HERE'S MY TRANSLATION.

WHAT DID THE SPY SAY?

MUNSHI: A SECRETARY OR WRITER.

THE COMPANY ADMINISTRATION COULDN'T FUNCTION WITHOUT SKILLED AND KNOWLEDGEABLE INDIAN EMPLOYEES.

BAKER ALI WAS A "CONFIDENTIAL MUNSHI," TRUSTED BY THE BRITISH GOVERNMENT.

THE COMPANY DEPENDS ON MY ADVICE AND LANGUAGE SKILLS. I HAVE SUCH AN IMPORTANT JOB.

SPYING ON MY OWN PEOPLE STINKS, BUT IT SURE PAYS WELL.

THEN

ONE DAY, BAKER ALI AND ANOTHER MUNSHI WERE APPROACHED BY AN INDIAN PRINCE NAMED MIRZA JUNGLY, WHO NEEDED A FAVOR.

PSST!

GRRR. I'M SO JEALOUS! MY BROTHER IS THE NAWAB OF AWADH. HE HAS ALL THE POWER AND I HAVE NONE.

A NAWAB, OR NABOB, IS A RULING PRINCE.

CAN YOU FIX IT SO THAT HE GETS INTO TROUBLE WITH THE BRITISH AND LOSES HIS TITLE? THEN I'LL BE THE NAWAB.

NO PROBLEM.

WE'LL INVENT A SPY PLOT!

THE TWO MUNSHIS WROTE DOZENS OF PHONY LETTERS STUFFED FULL OF DISINFORMATION THAT MADE MIRZA JUNGLY'S INNOCENT NAWAB BROTHER LOOK GUILTY AS SIN.

FAKE SECRET LETTERS IMPLICATING THE NAWAB WITH KNOWN ENEMIES OF THE BRITISH.

PLOTS

LETTERS HARASSING MERCHANTS

BRITISH BASHING LETTERS

THESE SHOULD GRAB THE COMPANY'S ATTENTION AND GET THEIR KNICKERS IN A TWIST.

THE LETTERS TWISTED COMPANY KNICKERS ALL RIGHT.

CRIKEY! A SPY PLOT. LET'S INVESTIGATE.

MIRZA JUNGLY WAS THRILLED. HIS BROTHER WAS BEING INVESTIGATED.

TITTER.

GIVE ME MORE MONEY OR I'LL TELL YOUR BROTHER.

BUT HE WAS NOT SO THRILLED WHEN MUNSHI BAKER ALI BLACKMAILED HIM.

THE BRITISH INTERVIEWED ALL THE KEY CONSPIRATORS AND SOME OF THE NAWAB'S FAMILY MEMBERS TOO.

NEXT.

BUT THE JIG WAS UP WHEN A RELATIVE POINTED THE FIRST FINGER ... AND THE FAMILY PLOT UNRAVELLED.

HE HELPED!

THERE'S NO SPY IN THIS FAMILY, JUST THAT TROUBLEMAKER.

BAKER ALI'S DIRECTOR BOSS WAS SHOCKED!

GASP.

BAKER ALI WAS TOSSED FROM HIS FANCY JOB.

GASP.

AND THE OTHER MUNSHI TOO.

MIRZA JUNGLY NEVER GOT TO BE THE NAWAB.

GASP.

Too bad for Mahomed Baker Ali and Mirza Jungly that a relative blew the whistle on the family's plot. But the trusted munshi's deliberate deception and disinformation plot was a huge shocker for the British East India Company and forced the British to debate these questions. How truthful or dependable is any intelligence that comes from outside spies or informants? How reliable is the work that is done in the writing office, which is manned by local munshis?

Half a century later, the company panicked anew about its lack of reliable intelligence when the Indian Rebellion of 1857 rocked the sub continent in a series of bitter and bloody revolts. The company finally wrestled back control, only to lose it when the British government stepped in and took over the job as rulers in 1858. India gained its independence from British rule in 1947.

WHACK A MOLE

Clueless Cold War spy chasers

Step right up, folks. It's Whack a Mole time! OK, this story has nothing to do with an old time carnival game, a man in a giant mole suit or even one of those tiny creatures that tunnel under a garden. It's about an espionage mole, which is the name given to insiders who sell their organization's or government's secrets to rivals. What dirty rats! I mean moles.

Holy Moley! Big events were happening in 1985. After 40 years of intense suspicions, down and dirty spying, dramatic secret agent captures and defections, the Cold War era was starting to thaw. (You remember the Cold War, right? Nuclear weapons threats between the Soviet Union and the West. Chilling stuff.) Anyway, in 1985, the Soviet Union wasn't doing very well economically and its people were no longer keen about their Union's politics (Communism). A new Soviet leader called Mikhail Gorbachev introduced reforms and more openness toward the West. Communism, the Soviet Union, and the Cold War would all be over within 6 years, but, of course, no one knew that at the time. So spies were still needed to sniff out one another's secret information.

Throughout the 1980s, the Soviet Union had no problems recruiting spies. Americans working for top-secret intelligence departments walked into Russian embassies offering to sell their nation's secrets for a price. These weasels, I mean, moles were all motivated by greed. Ready to read how the most highly paid and one of the most damaging moles in the USA's intelligence history got whacked?

So back to weasels, I mean moles. In the spring of 1985, a trusted man who worked for the USA's big spy organization, the Central Intelligence Agency (CIA), had second thoughts about where his loyalties lay and turned into a sneaky old mole. He became the most highly paid and most damaging mole in America's intelligence history. Will he be caught?

1985

WAS AN EXCELLENT

MOLE-WHACKING SPY-CATCHING YEAR.

BUT WILL THE **FBI** OR THE **CIA** CATCH THE NEW MOLE?

THE **FBI** (FEDERAL BUREAU OF INVESTIGATION) INCLUDES SPY-CATCHING UNDER ITS LIST OF DUTIES AS THE USA'S BIG CRIME SOLVER AND PROTECTOR OF THE NATION'S SECURITY.

THE **CIA** (CENTRAL INTELLIGENCE AGENCY) GATHERS INTELLIGENCE (VIA SPIES) FROM FOREIGN GOVERNMENTS, ANALYZES IT, THEN ADVISES USA'S GOVERNMENT AND MILITARY. WHAT ABOUT MOLE CATCHING? THE CIA'S COUNTER-INTELLIGENCE UNITS HANDLE THAT.

GOTCHA!

FBI

CIA

SQUEAK SQUEAK SQUEAK SQUEAK SQUEAK

A MOLE IS SOMEONE WHO WORKS FOR A GOVERNMENT OR AN ORGANIZATION AND STEALS THEIR SECRETS FOR THEIR RIVALS.

JUST A FEW OF THE SPIES CAUGHT IN 1985.

NABBED LARRY WU-TAI CHIN STARTED SNEAKING CIA SECRETS TO COMMUNIST CHINA IN 1952.

CAUGHT! RONALD PELTON SOLD HIS KNOWLEDGE OF THE USA'S TOP-SECRET SPY PLOT TO THE SOVIETS.

CAPTURED JOHN WALKER AND HIS SPY RING SNITCHED THE US NAVY'S COMMUNICATION SECRETS TO THE SOVIETS FROM 1968 TO 1985.

HMMM... WHO'S THIS?

SHHHH... I JUST BECAME A MOLE IN THE SPRING OF 1985. NO ONE SUSPECTS ME.

NAME: ALDRICH AMES JOB: A TRUSTED MID-LEVEL EMPLOYEE OF THE CIA (FOR 22 YEARS)

THE RUSSIANS WERE QUICK TO ACT ON ALDRICH'S INFORMATION.

1985-1986

ARREST THESE SPIES AND EXECUTE THEM.

WHAT SECRETS DID ALDRICH SELL? HE STARTED WITH A LIST OF AGENTS WHO WERE REPORTING SOVIET ACTIVITIES TO THE USA.

EXECUTED

MAJOR GENERAL DMITRI POLYAKOV
—THE CIA'S MOST VALUABLE SPY
—THE HIGHEST-RANKING MILITARY MAN IN SOVIET MILITARY INTELLIGENCE.

LIST

AND SEND THESE ONES TO PRISON.

EXECUTED

VALERY MARTYNOV

HE REVEALED THE IDENTITIES OF 50 SECRET SOVIET AGENTS WORKING OUT OF THE SOVIET EMBASSY.

ESCAPED

COLONEL OLEG GORDIEVSKY

HE SPIED AGAINST THE SOVIETS FOR BRITAIN'S MI6 ALDRICH RATTED ON HIM BUT THE BRITS GOT HIM TO SAFETY.

AT LEAST 10 AGENTS WERE EXECUTED.

THE CIA WERE QUICK TO MISS THEIR 8 AGENTS WHO HAD GONE... SILENT. THEY KNEW THIS MUST BE THE WORK OF AN INFORMER.

MISSING

ALL OF OUR IMPORTANT AGENTS HAVE BEEN TAKEN OUT OF ACTION. THIS MUST BE THE WORK OF THAT EX-CIA MOLE— EDWARD LEE HOWARD, WHO DEFECTED TO THE SOVIET UNION.

ON SECOND THOUGHT, NO. HOWARD NEVER KNEW THE NAMES OF ALL THESE MISSING AGENTS.

AFTER A WHILE, THE INVESTIGATION WAS DROPPED.

WE HAVE OTHER ASSIGNMENTS YOU KNOW.

TOP SECRET

BY THE WAY, ALDRICH WAS 1 OF ONLY 40 PEOPLE WHO KNEW THE NAMES OF ALL THOSE DEAD AGENTS.

BUT UH-OHH
ALDRICH HAD TO HAVE HIS ROUTINE LIE DETECTOR TEST. ALL CIA EMPLOYEES MUST HAVE 1 EVERY 5 YEARS.

RELAX, RELAX, RELAX...

1986

ALDRICH CONFIDED TO HIS SOVIET CONTACT...

THEY'RE GOING TO CATCH ME NOW.

IF YOU RELAX, YOU CAN FOOL THE LIE DETECTOR.

OK! YOU PASSED.

A LIE DETECTOR MEASURES THE BODY'S RESPONSES WHEN A QUESTION IS ASKED. STUFF LIKE BREATHING, SWEATING, AND HEARTBEATS.

ALDRICH RELAXED AND PASSED THE TEST.

THEN ALDRICH WAS SENT TO ITALY ON A NEW ASSIGNMENT.

I'LL BUY THIS AND THAT AND THAT...

1986-1991

FANCY NEW SUIT

I RE-MARRIED THEN TOLD EVERYONE THAT MY WIFE'S FAMILY WAS RICH.

ALDRICH'S NEW WIFE BOUGHT OVER 500 PAIRS OF SHOES AND 60 PURSES... HER LONG-DISTANCE PHONE CALLS COST OVER $6,000 A MONTH.

MEANWHILE IN 1988
THE FBI ANALYZED THE LOSS OF THEIR 2 IMPORTANT SOVIET AGENTS BACK IN 1985-86 AND FOR THE FIRST TIME THEY REALIZED...

OHHHH. THE CIA LOST 8 AGENTS AT THE SAME TIME THAT WE LOST OUR 2 AGENTS.

THERE MUST BE A MOLE IN THE CIA WHO HAS ACCESS TO FBI FILES.

I'VE GOT ANOTHER ASSIGNMENT NOW. GOTTA GO.

ME TOO.

BUT THE FBI DIDN'T INVESTIGATE WHO THE MOLE MIGHT BE. THE ANALYSIS TEAM BROKE UP AND MOVED ONTO NEW DUTIES.

Got him! But, sheesh! That traitor Aldrich Ames should have been captured much, much sooner. The FBI and the CIA reviewed how they had mishandled Aldrich's investigation and the United States government asked enough pointy questions to fill a 400-page report. After this spycatching bungle, which allowed a deadly mole to spy against the USA's intelligence operations for years, everyone had second thoughts.

If only the FBI and the CIA had shared their information with each other right from the start. If only the FBI and the CIA had investigated more thoroughly once they realized that those spy disappearances in 1985 and 1986 were the work of a mole. If only the CIA hadn't relied so heavily on lie detector tests. If, if, if ...

SOURCES

SOME OF THE SOURCES USED
TO RESEARCH THESE
SPY STORIES

BOOKS

Bayley, C.A. *Empire and Information: Intelligence Gathering and Social Communication in India, 1780—1870.* New York, NY: University of Cambridge Press, 1996.

Bazna, E. *I Was Cicero.* London: Andre Deutsch Ltd., 1962.

Chakraborty, G. *Espionage in Ancient India: From the Earliest Time to 12th Century A.D.* Calcutta, India: Minerva Associates, 1990.

Crowdy, T. *The Enemy Within: A History of Espionage.* Oxford and New York: Osprey, 2006.

Dewing, H. B. (translator). *Procopius: History of the Wars of Justinian* (Loeb Classical Library Edition). Cambridge: Harvard University Press, 1943.

Garcia-Arenal, M. *Ahmad al-Mansur: The Beginnings of Modern Morocco.* Oxford: Oneworld Publications, 2009.

Greenfield, A. B. *A Perfect Red: Empire, Espionage and the Quest for the Color of Desire.* New York: HarperCollins, 2005.

Hearn, C. G. *Spies & Espionage: A Directory.* San Diego, CA: Thunder Bay Press, 2006.

Khan, D. *The Codebreakers: The Story of Secret Writing.* New York: MacMillan, 1967.

Manning, C.S. *Ancient and Medieval India.* London: Wm. H. Allen & Co., 1869.

Marks, L. *Between Silk and Cyanide: A Codemaker's War, 1941-1945.* New York: Free Press, 1999.

Moyzisch, L.C. *Operation Cicero.* New York: Pyramid, 1958.

Persico, J. E. *Piercing the Reich: The Penetration of Nazi Germany by American Secret Agents During World War II.* New York: Viking Press, 1979.

Richelson, J. T. *Century of Spies: Intelligence in the Twentieth Century.* New York: Oxford University Press, 1995.

Richelson, J. *The Wizards of Langley: Inside the CIA's Directorate of Science and Technology.* Boulder, Colo: Westview Press. 2001.

Rigden, D. *How to be a spy: The World War II SOE Training Manual.* Toronto, Canada: Dundurn Press, 2004.

Sawyer, R.D. and Sawyer, M.L. *The Tao of Spycraft: Intelligence and Practice in Traditional China.* Boulder, Colo.: Westview Press, 1998.

Sheldon, R.M. *Espionage in the Ancient World: An Annotated Bibliography of Books and Articles in Western Languages.* Jefferson, N.C: McFarland & Co., 2003.

MORE BOOKS

The *Sunday Times* Insight Team, *Rainbow Warrior: The French Attempt to sink Greenpeace.* London: Century Hutchinson Ltd., 1986.

Turtledove, H. (introduction, notes and translation) *The Chronicle of Theophanes: An English Translation of Anni Mundi 6095-6305 (A.D. 602-813).* Philadelphia, Pa.: University of Pennsylvania Press, 1982.

Wilson, J. A. *"The Texts of the Battle of Kadesh" :The American Journal of Semitic Languages and Literatures.* Chicago, Ill.: University of Chicago Press, 1927.

DOCUMENTS

Document 27. Memorandum for: [deleted] Views on Trained Cats [deleted] for [deleted] Use. Declassified and partly censored CIA, Science and Technology Directorate document released in September, 1983. USA.

Document C05301269. Project Azorian: The Story of the Hughes Glomar Explorer. Declassified and partly censored CIA document released on January 4, 2010. USA.

A Review of the FBI's Performance in Uncovering the Espionage Activities of Aldrich Hazen Ames (April 1997). An unclassified executive summary by the Office of the Inspector General, Department of Justice, USA. 1997.

WEBSITES

christchurchcitylibraries.com/Kids/NZDisasters/RainbowWarrior.asp
The *Rainbow Warrior* bombing

www.bbc.co.uk/history/british/empire_seapower/east_india_01.shtml
An overview of the British East India Trading Company

www.bbc.co.uk/history/worldwars/wwtwo/soe_training_01.shtml
The training of allied spies in World War II

www.mi5.gov.uk/output/carl-hans-lody.html
A case history of the WWI German spy, Carl Hans Lody

ABOUT THE AUTHOR-ILLUSTRATOR OF THIS BOOK

TINA HOLDCROFT

HAS ILLUSTRATED ZILLIONS OF PICTURES FOR BOOKS, MAGAZINES, ADVERTISING, AND CORPORATE STUFF FOR A QUARTER OF A CENTURY.

SPY, SPY AGAIN
IS THE THIRD BOOK THAT TINA HAS AUTHORED.

For my dad Cyril, who gave me his daft DNA.
—T.H.

A sincere thank-you to expert reader Wesley Wark, professor at the
Munk School of Global Affairs, University of Toronto.

We acknowledge the support of the Canada Council for the Arts, the Ontario Arts
Council, and the Government of Canada through the Canada Book Fund (CBF) for
our publishing activities.

 ONTARIO ARTS COUNCIL
CONSEIL DES ARTS DE L'ONTARIO

Cataloging in Publication

Holdcroft, Tina
        Spy, spy again : true tales of failed espionage / written and illustrated by Tina
Holdcroft.

ISBN 978-1-55451-223-2 (bound).—ISBN 978-1-55451-222-5 (pbk.)

        1. Espionage—History—Juvenile literature.
2. Spies—History—Juvenile literature. I. Title.

UB270.5.H65 2011   j327.12   C2010-907840-3

Distributed in Canada by:
Firefly Books Ltd.
66 Leek Crescent
Richmond Hill, ON
L4B 1H1

Published in the U.S.A. by Annick Press (U.S.) Ltd.
Distributed in the U.S.A. by:
Firefly Books (U.S.) Inc.
P.O. Box 1338
Ellicott Station
Buffalo, NY 14205

Printed in Canada.

Visit us at: www.annickpress.com
Visit Tina Holdcroft at: www.tinaholdcroft.com

MIX
Paper from
responsible sources
FSC® C011825